Being Healthy, Feeling Great

Diet

Angela Royston

New York

Published in 2010 by The Rosen Publishing Group Inc.
29 East 21st Street, New York, NY 10010

First Edition

Design: Nick Leggett and Paul Myerscough
Editor: Sarah Eason
Picture research: Maria Joannou
Illustrator: Geoff Ward
Consultant: Sue Beck MSc, BSc
Commissioning Editor for Wayland: Jennifer Sanderson

Library of Congress Cataloging-in-Publication Data

Royston, Angela.
Diet / Angela Royston.
p. cm. -- (Being healthy, feeling great)
Includes index.
ISBN 978-1-61532-367-8 (library binding)
ISBN 978-1-61532-372-2 (paperback)
ISBN 978-1-61532-373-9 (6-pack)
1. Nutrition--Juvenile literature. I. Title.
RA784.R697 2010
613.2--dc22

2009023887

Photographs:
The publisher would like to thank the following for permission to reproduce photographs:
Alamy Images: Ace Stock Ltd 26, Elvele Images Ltd/Alexandra Carlile 5, Kuttig People 25; Corbis:
Giulio Di Mauro/EPA 24, Kevin Dodge 10, Randy Faris 27, Erin Ryan/Zefa 23; Istockphoto:
Aleaimage 28l, Wendell Franks 28t, Steven Miric 28r; Rex Features: Martin Lee 4; Shutterstock:
Andi Berger 20, Stephanie Connell 8, Elena Elisseeva 14, Christopher Elwell 7, Gelpi 15, Robert
Gubbins 19, Bjorn Heller 17, Stephen Mcsweeny 16, Paulaphoto 12, Vladimir Sazonov 21, Andrey
Shadrin 1, 11, David P. Smith 13, Jozsef Szasz-Fabian 18, Tihis 9, 31, Graca Victoria 22.
Cover: Shutterstock/Stephen McSweeny.

Manufactured in China

CPSIA Compliance Information: Batch #WAW0102PK: For Further Information
contact Rosen Publishing, New York, New York at 1-800-237-9932

Contents

Why do you need to eat?

Food is essential for life. It gives you energy, and it contains nutrients that you need to grow and be healthy. Your body breaks down and digests the nutrients in food. Your blood then carries them to every part of your body.

When you are hungry

You feel hungry when your stomach is empty and your body is low on energy. When you are hungry, the smell of food makes your mouth water with extra saliva. When you eat, your teeth chew each mouthful of food. The saliva mixes with the food to make a mushy ball, which you swallow.

Food gives you the energy you need to lead an active and healthy life.

Digesting

The food you swallow goes into your stomach. Here, special acids mix with it and turn it into a kind of thick "soup." This then slowly passes into your small intestine, where it is broken up into separate nutrients. The nutrients are so tiny that they pass through the walls of the small intestine into the blood. The rest passes on through the large intestine and becomes solid waste, called feces.

Nutrients

Nutrients are chemicals that your body needs. For instance, foods such as bread are rich in carbohydrates. Your body uses the carbohydrates for energy. All the parts of your body, from your hair to your bones, are made of different proteins. Some foods, such as fish, contain lots of protein. Your body uses proteins from food to make the proteins in your body. A healthy, balanced diet should contain all the nutrients your body needs.

Your body needs nutrients to perform activities, such as running.

Amazing fact

Most food stays in your mouth for less than a minute, but it can stay in your stomach for up to four hours. It can then take another 20 hours to pass through your small and large intestines. This is because your intestines are very long— about three times as long as your height from head to toe.

A balancing act

The food you normally eat is called your diet. To eat healthily, you need to eat most of your food from four main food groups: carbohydrates; fruit and vegetables; protein; and dairy food. You can also eat a small amount of food from a fifth food group: sugar and fat.

Carbohydrates

Cereals and potatoes are starchy foods that contain carbohydrates. Cereals are grains, such as wheat, oats, and rice. Breakfast cereals are made from grains. Wheat is used to make pasta and bread. You should aim to eat five portions of starchy carbohydrates a day.

Fruit and vegetables

Fruit and vegetables contain lots of vitamins, minerals, and fiber (see pages 16–19). Fresh, raw fruit and vegetables contain the most nutrients, but cooked, frozen, dried, and canned vegetables are good, too. You should eat at least five portions of fruit and vegetables a day.

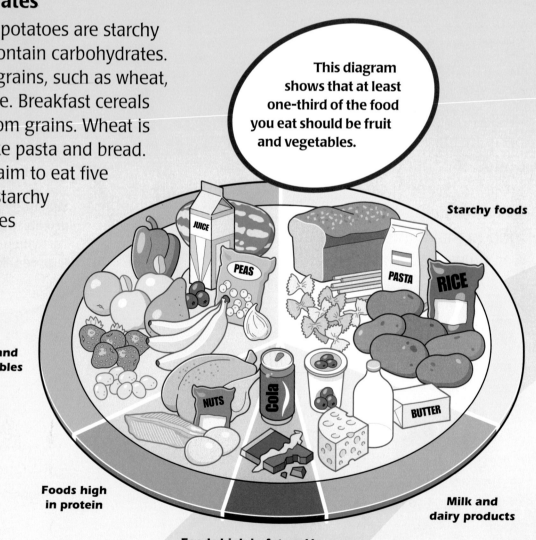

This diagram shows that at least one-third of the food you eat should be fruit and vegetables.

JUICE

PEAS

Starchy foods

PASTA

RICE

Fruit and vegetables

NUTS

Cola

BUTTER

Foods high in protein

Milk and dairy products

Foods high in fat and/or sugar

Weigh it up

One portion of food weighs 2.8 oz. (80 g).

Tomatoes and salad vegetables can make sandwiches much healthier.

Meat, fish, and alternatives

Meat and fish contain protein. Some people, called vegetarians, do not eat meat or fish. Instead, they eat foods such as eggs, nuts, and beans to give them the protein they need. These are tasty foods for everyone. Try to eat two or three portions of protein a day.

Dairy food

Dairy food is milk and food made from milk, such as cheese and yogurt. Dairy food contains protein, as well as important vitamins and minerals. A healthy diet includes two or three portions of dairy foods a day.

Sugar and fat

Some foods, such as fruit, contain natural sugar. Sugar is added to other foods, such as cakes, to make them taste sweet. If you crave a little of something sweet, fruit is a much healthier choice than cake.

Many types of food contain fat. For example, beef may have streaks of fat running through it. You need to include a small amount of fat in your diet. Some fats, such as olive oil, are healthier than others. Choose these whenever you can.

Food for energy

Bread is a carbohydrate, which contains lots of starch. If you chew a piece of bread, you will notice that it begins to taste sweet. That is because your saliva changes some of the starch in the bread into sugar. Your body breaks down the rest of the starch inside your body. It turns it into glucose, which is a kind of sugar, and this then goes into your blood. The blood carries the glucose and other nutrients to every part of your body. This gives you energy.

Using energy

Every activity you do uses energy. You need energy to move around, to think—and even to sleep. Most of your energy is needed for physical exercise. People who are very active need to eat more starchy carbohydrates. Professional football players and other athletes often eat starchy foods, such as pasta, a few hours before they take part in a game or competition.

Rice and pasta contain plenty of starch, which gives you energy.

Energy burst

Always try to wash your hands before you eat. Sometimes, this may not be possible—especially if you are in the middle of exercise. Then, a banana is really handy. It gives you energy—and you can eat it without touching it with your fingers!

Energy dips

You may begin to feel tired a few hours after eating. This is because your body has digested all the starchy food you have eaten by then, and your blood is running low on glucose. This tired feeling is often called an "energy dip" (or "energy slump").

A healthy snack to top up your energy will make you feel better. Dried fruit, such as dates, is a good snack. Fruit contains natural sugar, which your body digests quickly. This gives you an instant burst of energy. A banana is a great snack, because it contains starch as well as sugar. This makes your energy last even longer.

Eating a banana can help to keep your energy levels high.

9

Beware of sugar

Sugar is used to sweeten soft drinks, cookies, cakes, candy, and other sweet food. Without sugar, these foods and drinks would not taste that nice. Lots of people enjoy sugary foods because sugar tastes good and gives them energy. However, for many reasons, sugar is not a healthy choice.

Sugar highs

When you eat or drink sweet things, the sugar in them goes straight into your blood. This gives you an instant burst of energy, called a "sugar high," which can make you hyperactive. When someone is hyperactive, they find it hard to sit still and concentrate.

Energy from sugar does not last long, and a sugar high is soon followed by an energy dip. An energy dip makes you feel tired and bad-tempered. If you need a burst of energy, it is much better to eat fruit. Fruit contains other nutrients and fiber, as well as sugar, and keeps you going for longer.

An energy dip can suddenly make you feel very tired.

Tooth decay

Some of the sugar in sweet foods and drinks stays in your mouth after you have swallowed. The sugar clings to your teeth and gums. Bacteria in your mouth feed on the sugar and produce a kind of acid, which then attacks your teeth. The acid can make holes in your teeth. This is called tooth decay and it can be painful.

The bacteria in your mouth also produce a white, sticky substance, called plaque. Plaque makes your breath smell bad. It can also cause gum disease. You can protect your teeth and gums by brushing them well. It is best to do this at least twice a day: morning and night.

Healthy Hints

Avoid sugar

You can also protect your teeth even more by eating less sugar. If you do eat or drink something sugary, try to brush your teeth shortly afterward. If this is not possible, drink some water to help wash the sugar out of your mouth.

The natural sugar in fruit is much healthier than sugar added to candy and cookies.

Protein: the body's building blocks

Proteins are essential for good health. Hair, skin, muscles, and other parts of the body are all made of different kinds of protein. Some foods are very rich in proteins. It is good to eat a variety of these protein-rich foods, so that your body is as healthy as possible.

Protein-rich foods

Meat, chicken, and fish contain all the protein your body needs. You can choose from different kinds of meat, including beef, lamb, pork, rabbit, and venison. Some meat, such as beef and lamb, contains a lot of fat. If you eat too much of the type of fat found in meat, it can be unhealthy. It is good to eat different kinds of meat, rather than just one kind. Try to eat chicken and other poultry, such as turkey, too.

Protein builds healthy hair, skin, and muscles.

A healthy diet should include one to two portions of protein every day.

Fish is especially good for your body because it does not contain much fat. Some fish, such as mackerel and sardines, are called oily fish. These are very healthy because they contain omega oils and other important nutrients that are good for you.

Vegetarian protein

Vegetarians eat cheese, nuts, and pulses to get the proteins they need. Pulses include beans, chickpeas, and lentils. Some vegetarians eat eggs, too. Vegetarian protein is not as complete as meat or fish protein. This means that it does not contain all the different types of protein your body needs in just one type of food. By eating two different kinds of vegetarian protein, you can make it more complete. For instance, you can eat a nut burger with cheese. This gives you all the protein you need.

Healthy Hints

No to salt

Peanuts contain lots of protein. However, salted peanuts contain up to four times as much salt as meat or chicken. Too much salt is bad for your health, so choose unsalted peanuts instead of salted ones.

Go easy on the fats

Fat is found naturally in some foods, such as meat and avocados. Butter contains a lot of fat and so does oil, such as corn oil. People often use butter and oil in cooking.

It is important to include some fat in your diet because fat gives you energy. It also helps your body to absorb some of the vitamins it needs.

Just a little

You need to eat only a small amount of fat. If you eat too much, when your body has taken all the energy it needs, the rest of the fat is stored as "body fat." A little body fat is healthy, but too much fat can be unhealthy.

Good fat, bad fat

There are three main kinds of fat. Unsaturated fats are the healthiest and are better for you than saturated fats and trans-fats.

Babies and children need to eat more fat because they are growing quickly.

Saturated fats or trans-fats are often found in fast foods and in foods such as sausages, cakes, and cookies. These types of fat are unhealthy because they can increase the amount of cholesterol in your blood. Over time, this can block your blood vessels and lead to heart disease.

Unsaturated fats are found in oily fish, avocados, nuts, and seeds. Certain types of oil, such as olive oil and sunflower oil, also contain unsaturated fats. Unsaturated fats reduce the amount of cholesterol in your blood and protect you from heart disease, so they are a better choice than saturated fats.

Omega oils

It is important to eat some foods that contain omega oils because they keep your blood flowing around your body. Nuts and oily fish are good choices. Omega oils in fish have an added benefit, too—people believe that they make your brain work better.

Amazing fact

Everyone needs a little body fat. Body fat keeps you warm, and is a good food store for emergencies. If you are sick and cannot eat, your body breaks down some of your body fat to give you energy until you can eat again.

Rich, frosted cakes may be tasty, but they are full of saturated fat.

Vitamins and minerals

Vitamins and minerals are very important nutrients for good health. The great news is that, apart from sugar, most foods contain some vitamins or minerals. Eating a wide variety of foods will give you all you need.

Vitamins

Every part of your body uses vitamins. Vitamins are known by letters of the alphabet. For example, vitamin A keeps your skin, hair, and nails healthy.

There are several kinds of vitamin B, such as B6 and B12. They all help you get energy from food. Vitamin C helps wounds to heal, and vitamin K makes your blood clot. Vitamin E helps you fight illness and disease.

Minerals

Two of the most important minerals are calcium and iron. Calcium makes your bones and teeth strong and it helps your muscles to work. Milk and dairy products contain lots of calcium and other important minerals. Meat and sardines are rich in iron. Iron helps your blood take in oxygen. If you are low in iron, you may feel tired and sick.

Milk is an excellent source of calcium for young people.

Salt

Another name for salt is sodium, which is another kind of mineral. Your body needs some salt to work properly. Salt occurs naturally in many foods. However, many people eat much more salt than their body needs. Some people add salt to food when they are cooking or to their finished meal. Ready-made meals usually contain a lot of salt to make them taste better. Potato chips and salted nuts are high in salt, too. If you like eating lots of these types of food, you are probably eating too much salt. You should eat no more than one teaspoon of salt a day.

True taste

Salt hides the true taste of food. If you stop adding salt to your food, you will soon be able to enjoy its real taste. If you want extra flavor, try adding lemon juice or herbs and spices instead.

Potato chips are tasty and convenient but they contain more salt than is good for you.

Regular fiber

Fiber is the parts of fruit, vegetables, and grains that your body cannot digest. It includes the husk of grains of wheat and the stringy parts of fruit and vegetables. Fiber is not a nutrient, but you need it to be healthy.

What fiber does for you

Fiber helps your digestive system to work well. It is tough, so you need to chew it for longer. Chewing makes the rest of your food easier to digest. Fiber cannot be digested, so it makes your feces softer and bulkier. That makes it easier to push feces out of your body. If your diet is low in fiber, food will take longer to pass through your body. Your feces may become dry, making it difficult to get rid of. This is called constipation.

Dried apricots, dates, raisins, and figs are rich in fiber and are all good food choices.

The stringy parts of celery are fiber. They help your digestive system to work well.

Foods rich in fiber

Vegetables are one of the best sources of fiber. Carrots, cabbage, broccoli, and celery all contain lots of it. So do beans, lentils, peas, and dried fruit, such as currants, figs, and dates. Whole-wheat bread and whole-grain food, such as brown rice and whole-wheat pasta, are made with the whole grain, including the husk. They are high in fiber and are much healthier than white bread, white rice, and food made with white flour.

Healthy Hints

Beet test

One way to tell whether your diet contains enough fiber is to eat a portion of beets. You can tell when the fiber from beets has passed through your body because it stains your feces red. This should happen between 12 and 24 hours after eating the beets. If this takes longer, you probably need to eat more fiber.

19

Water

Drinking water is very important because it helps to keep your body healthy. Two-thirds of your body is made up of water. Body fluids, such as blood and digestive juices, are mainly water. Your brain, muscles, and other parts of your body contain water, too. You lose water all the time, as sweat and urine, in feces and when you breathe out. To replace the water you lose, you should drink five or six 8-oz. glasses (1.25–1.5 liters) of water or other liquids a day.

Feeling thirsty

If you do not drink enough liquid, you become dehydrated. When you are dehydrated, you may suffer from headaches, lack of concentration, tiredness, and dizziness. You may find it hard to sleep properly. Usually, when your body is short of water, you feel thirsty and so you drink something. However, you can be dehydrated without feeling thirsty. This is why it is important to drink regularly throughout the day, whether you feel thirsty or not.

Drinking tap water or filtered water is just as good as drinking expensive bottled water.

Other drinks

Fruit juice, milk, and weak tea are mainly water. These are good choices for your five to six glasses of liquid a day. However, cola and coffee do not count because they contain caffeine. Caffeine makes your kidneys work faster so you lose more water than you should.

Juicy fruits, such as watermelon, contain lots of water. Eating them will top up the water in your body.

Water balance

Your kidneys control the amount of water in your body. They clean your blood, removing some of the water and any substances your body does not need to make urine. The urine is stored in your bladder, until you empty it when you urinate. You can tell if you are drinking enough liquid because you should need to urinate once every two or three hours. If you do not urinate this often, you need to drink more.

21

Eating too much

To be as healthy as possible, it helps to be at the right body weight for your height. To maintain a healthy weight, you need to eat the right amount of food. It helps to do exercise, too. If you regularly eat more food that you need to, your body will store body fat. You will gradually become overweight.

Keep fit

Exercise helps people to stay at the right weight. To be fit and healthy, 11-year-olds need one hour's exercise a day. Walking, cycling, running, and swimming are great choices.

Obesity

Some people are obese. This means that they are very overweight. People who are obese can have some very serious health problems, such as heart disease, diabetes, and cancer. Some people who are obese may also feel unhappy about the way they look and feel.

Losing weight

It is possible to lose weight and to get to a healthy weight. If you are overweight, it may take a little effort but the results are worth it. When people lose weight, they often feel fitter, healthier, and happier. A doctor or nutritionist can help people to lose weight by giving them information about what to do.

Fast foods may taste good but they can make people overweight.

Making healthy food choices is the first step to reaching a healthy weight. Cutting out, or cutting down on, sweet and fatty foods is a great idea. Instead of eating sweets, you can eat fruit. Instead of using butter, you can use low-fat spreads. Instead of snacking on potato or tortilla chips, try snacking on vegetables. Eating food that is rich in fiber helps you to feel full more quickly. You eat less, because you feel less hungry.

Dieting

Some people go on special diets to lose weight really quickly. This can be very unhealthy. Some diets do not provide all the nutrients you need. When you lose weight too quickly, you often gain the weight again, as soon as you finish the diet. This is called "yo-yo" dieting. By eating healthily most of the time, you can avoid this type of dieting and maintain a healthy weight.

Eating too little

Eating too little can bring as many problems as eating too much. If people do not eat enough, they cannot get all the nutrients they need. Seriously underweight people can become ill.

Signs and symptoms

When people do not eat enough, they lose weight and become thin. People who are underweight often have acne, especially on their back. Their hair becomes thinner and some of it may fall out. They may feel very tired and they do not have the energy they need to do everyday things, such as going to school or going out with friends.

Many people think that photographs of very thin models encourage anorexia.

Healthy Hints

Think positively

Sometimes, people see faults in themselves that no one else can see. They think they are fat when they are not. Try to see yourself as others do. If they say that you look good, believe them.

Eating disorders

Sometimes, people have an eating disorder, such as anorexia or bulimia. More and more people, including both boys and girls, are suffering from eating disorders. They want to be thin, because they think that this is attractive. However, they often have the wrong idea about how they look. They may be a healthy weight but think that they are fat. They take extreme action to lose weight. People who have eating disorders urgently need help from a doctor.

People who suffer from anorexia do not eat enough. They may eat a little fruit and salad, but they avoid carbohydrates, protein, sugar, and fat. They think these foods will make them fat.

People who suffer from bulimia often eat plenty of food. However, they make themselves vomit or they use laxatives soon after they have eaten, so that the food does not make them put on weight.

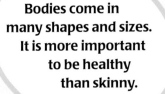

Bodies come in many shapes and sizes. It is more important to be healthy than skinny.

A healthy diet

A balanced diet is a healthy diet, where a variety of foods are eaten every day.

How much food do people need?

Boys and men are usually taller and heavier than girls and women of the same age. Because of this, they need to eat more to make sure that they get all the energy they need. Children and young people need lots of nutrients, because they are growing.

Therefore, they need to eat more than adults, who have reached their final height.

People who exercise a lot also need to eat more than others, because exercise burns energy more quickly than other activities. Often, as people become older, they are less active. This is why older people often eat less than young people.

Healthy or unhealthy?

Which of these foods are healthy choices? Which are unhealthy?

Whole-wheat bread
Hot dogs
Soft drinks
Sugary cereals
Fresh fruit salad
Vegetables and pasta
Milk
Fast-food burgers

People who eat healthily all their lives are more likely to stay fit and healthy when they get older.

Choosing healthy foods

Food is healthiest when it is natural. Fresh fruit is healthier than a fruit snack bar. Pork chops are healthier than sausages. Processed foods often have added ingredients and some of them may not be good for you.

For instance, beans are a healthy source of protein. Baked beans from a can are not quite as healthy, because they may have added sugar or salt. It is easy to eat too much salt, sugar, and fat when you eat lots of processed food.

Healthy Hints

Checking food labels

You can read food labels on processed food packaging to see exactly what is in the food. Food labels tell you at a glance how much carbohydrate, protein, fat, sugar, and salt food contains. They can help you to make the healthiest choices.

If you do eat junk food occasionally, try to make sure you eat healthily the rest of the time.

Make a healthy pizza!

Pizzas are delicious but they are often made using unhealthy ingredients. Here is a quick, easy way to make your own healthy pizza! This pizza uses whole-wheat pita bread for the base, for extra fiber. Add your own favorite extras to the healthy cheese and tomato topping.

Safety note: ask an adult to help you when you put your pizza in the oven.

Ingredients for four pizzas

For the base:
4 whole-wheat pita breads

For the topping:
1 can of chopped tomatoes
3.5 oz. (100 g) grated cheese (choose reduced-fat Cheddar or Parmesan, if you can)

Topping extras:
Choose your favorites from these healthy foods:

Protein-rich extras:
Ham, tuna, shrimp, cooked chicken, pine nuts, mozzarella.

Fruit and vegetable extras:
Sliced red or green peppers, olives, pineapple, spinach, sliced onion.

How to prepare your pizza

1 Heat the oven to 400°F (200°C).

2 Cover the pita breads with a layer of chopped tomatoes, followed by a layer of grated cheese.

3 Now add your favorite topping extras. Include at least one choice from protein-rich extras and one choice from fruit and vegetable extras.

4 Sprinkle a layer of grated cheese across the top of the pizza.

5 Put the pizza in the oven. Bake for 20 minutes. Remove and enjoy when it is cool enough to eat!

Quiz

How healthy is the food you eat? Try this quick quiz to find out.

1 You have slept too long, and you are running late for school. Do you:

a) Skip breakfast?

b) Grab a doughnut on your way to school?

c) Quickly drink a glass of milk and take a banana or a slice of bread to eat on the way?

2 You are really thirsty. Which of these drinks are you most likely to buy:

a) A carton of juice?

b) A can of soda?

c) A bottle of water?

3 You are eating out. Which option would you choose:

a) Spaghetti, followed by ice cream?

b) Burger and fries, followed by chocolate cake?

c) Fish with vegetables, followed by fruit?

4 You are hungry when you get home from school. Do you:

a) Have some more breakfast cereal?

b) Grab a bag of potato chips and a chocolate cookie?

c) Chop up some fruit and vegetables to dip into yogurt or hummus?

5 You decide to make a meal for your family. Do you:

a) Heat up some frozen pizzas and serve them with salad?

b) Heat up a ready-made meal from the supermarket?

c) Cook some chicken or lentils with vegetables and serve with rice?

Answers

Mostly **as**. You often choose the easy option, which may be unhealthy. Try to practice healthier habits.

Mostly **bs**. Oh dear! You still need to think about healthy eating. At the moment, you are choosing unhealthy foods. Try reading this book again to get some more ideas.

Mostly **cs**. Very good! You are choosing healthy food that will help you feel good and look good! If you want to find out more, trying looking at the books and websites on page 31.

Glossary

acne A skin problem that causes pimples on the face or body.

anorexia An eating disorder in which people restrict what they eat because they think they are too fat.

bacteria Organisms that can only be seen through a microscope. Bacteria can cause disease.

bulimia An eating disorder in which people vomit or use laxatives after eating because they think they are too fat.

calcium A mineral found in some foods, especially milk.

digestive system Parts of the body that digest food and absorb it into the blood.

eating disorder A condition, such as anorexia and bulimia, in which people eat unhealthily.

fiber The substance found in some foods that travels through the digestive system quickly and easily.

food groups Groups of foods that contain similar nutrients; there are five main food groups.

husk The outer covering of cereal grains.

iron A mineral found in some foods, such as beef and spinach.

large intestine The part of the digestive system that produces feces.

laxatives Substances that help to get feces out of someone's body.

minerals Healthy substances, such as iron, found in some foods.

nutrients Parts of food that your body uses to get energy and to work properly.

nutritionist A person who advises what people should eat to be healthy.

omega oil The oil found in some fish, nuts, and seeds, which is essential to good health.

processed food Food that has been changed from its natural state.

proteins Nutrients found in some foods, such as meat and fish.

saturated fats Animal fat.

small intestine The part of the digestive system in which food is digested and absorbed into the blood.

trans-fats Unhealthy fats found in some foods, such as margarine.

unsaturated fats Oil or fat that comes from plants.

urinate When you pee.

urine Pee.

vitamins Chemicals found in some foods, which the body needs to be healthy.

Find out more and Web Sites

Books

Healthy Eating: Diet and Nutrition by Anna Claybourne (Heinemann Educational Books, 2008)

Making Healthy Choices: Food for Sports by Neil Morris (Heinemann Educational Books, 2006)

Why Should I Eat This Carrot? And Other Questions About Healthy Eating by Louise Spilsbury (Topeka Bindery, 2003)

Web Sites

Due to the changing nature of Internet links, PowerKids Press has developed an online list of Web sites related to the subject of this book. This site is updated regularly. Please use this link to access this list: http://www.powerkidslinks.com/bhfg/diet/

Index